W9-AYI-537

If I Lived In Japan . . .

By Rosanne Knorr
Illustrated by John Knorr

LONGSTREET PRESS, INC.
Atlanta, Georgia

Also by Rosanne and John Knorr

If I Lived In France . . .

If I Lived In Spain . . .

If I Lived In Germany . . .

Join me for a visit
To a far Asian land.
See what life would be like
If you lived in Japan.

KONNICHI WA

If I Lived In Japan . . .

Published by
LONGSTREET PRESS, INC.
A subsidiary of Cox Newspapers,
A subsidiary of Cox Enterprises, Inc.
2140 Newmarket Parkway
Suite 118
Marietta, GA 30067

Copyright © 1995 by Rosanne Knorr
Illustrations © by John Knorr

All rights reserved. No part of this book may be reproduced in any form or by any means without the prior written permission of the Publisher, excepting brief quotations used in connection with reviews, written specifically for inclusion in a magazine or newspaper.

Printed in the United States of America

1st printing 1995

Library of Congress Catalog Card Number: 95-77261

ISBN 1-56352-236-5

This book was printed by Horowitz/Rae, Fairfield, NJ

Electronic film prep and separations by Advertising Technologies, Inc., Atlanta, GA

Jacket design by Neil Hollingsworth
Book Design by Jill Dible

Special thanks to Elizabeth Baldwin, Virginia Murray, Nobuaki Oda, Seigakuin Atlanta International School, Keiko Scott and the Japanese Consulate, Atlanta, for their help in ensuring the accuracy of Japanese translations, pronunciations and customs.

If I lived in Japan,
I'd speak a new way.
The language I know
Is called *Nihongo*.

Japanese word:	Sounds like. . .	And it means. . .
Nihongo	nee-hohn-go	Japanese
Wakarimasu ka?	wah-car-e-mahs ka	Do you understand?
Hai	hi	Yes

I'm out and about.
Now who do I see?
It's my very best friend.
Konnichi wa! Genki?

Japanese word:	Sounds like. . .	And it means. . .
Konnichi wa!	kohn-nee-chee-wah	Hello
Genki?	gen-kee	How are you?

He asks me the same.
"Hai," I say, *"yes."*
Since I'm doing well,
I say, *"Genki desu."*

Japanese word:	Sounds like. . .	And it means. . .
Hai	hi	Yes
Genki desu	gen-kee dess	I'm fine.

With a wave of my hand,
I yell, "See you later."
"*Sayōnara*," I say
As I go on my way.

Japanese word:	Sounds like. . .	And it means. . .
Sayōnara	sah-o-nah-lah	Goodbye

ANATA NO NAMAE WA?
YOSHIO

Who am I? What's my name?
It's easy to know.
Just read the name tag
That I wear to *gakkō*.

Japanese word:	Sounds like. . .	And it means. . .
gakkō	gah-ko	school
Anata no namae wa?	ahna-ta no nah-ma-eh wah	What's your name?
Yoshio	yo-she-o	Yoshio

What month does school start?
I'll give you a clue.
It's fourth in the year
And called *Shi-gatsu*.

Japanese word:	Sounds like...	And it means...	Japanese word:	Sounds like...	And it means...
Ichi-gatsu	echee-gaht-su	January	*Go-gatsu*	go-gaht-su	May
Ni-gatsu	ne-gaht-su	February	*Roku-gatsu*	roh-koo-gaht-su	June
San-gatsu	sahn-gaht-su	March	*Shichi-gatsu*	she-chee-gaht-su	July
Shi-gatsu	she-gaht-su	April			

ZAIMASU

To start the school day
We all bow to *sensei*.
The more respect that I show,
The lower I go.

Japanese word:	Sounds like...	And it means...	Japanese word:	Sounds like...	And it means...
Hachi-gatsu	hah-chee-gaht-su	August	*Juni-gatsu*	joo-nee-gaht-su	December
Ku-gatsu	koo-gaht-su	September	*Karenda*	kal-en-dah	calendar
Ju-gatsu	joo-gaht-su	October	*sensei*	sen-say	teacher
Juichi-gatsu	joo-echee-gaht-su	November	*Ohayo gozaimasu*	ohio-go-zy-e-mahs	Good morning

I draw words like pictures,
Using ink and a brush. See!
This one means "tree."
We call our symbols *kanji*.

Japanese word:	Sounds like. . .	And it means. . .
kanji	kahn-jee	Japanese symbols

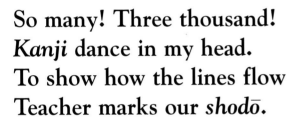

So many! Three thousand!
Kanji dance in my head.
To show how the lines flow
Teacher marks our *shodō*.

Japanese word:	Sounds like. . .	And it means. . .
shodō	sho-doh	calligraphy

Math class studies numbers,
One, two, three and four.
But when you listen to me,
It's **"Ichi, ni, san, shi."**

1-ICHI	6-ROKU
2-NI	7-SHICHI
3-SAN	8-HACHI
4-SHI	9-KYU
5-GO	10-JŪ

Japanese word:	Sounds like. . .	And it means. . .	Japanese word:	Sounds like. . .	And it means. . .
ichi	e-chee	one	*roku*	low-koo	six
ni	nee	two	*shichi*	she-chee	seven
san	sahn	three	*hachi*	hah-chee	eight
shi	she	four	*kyu*	kyoo	nine
go	go	five	*jū*	joo	ten

I'm hungry. Aren't you?
Let's eat *chūshoku*.
If I'm good as can be,
I might get a *kukkii*.

Japanese word:	Sounds like. . .	And it means. . .
chūshoku	choo-sho-koo	lunch
kukkii	kuk-kee	cookie

No doubt, I am busy
Right through *Do-yōbi*.
But this music is fun
So I like my *ressun*.

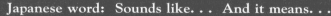

Japanese word:	Sounds like. . .	And it means. . .	Japanese word:	Sounds like. . .	And it means. . .
ressun	reh-sun	lesson/practice	*Sui-yōbi*	soo-e-yoh-be	Wednesday
Nichi-yōbi	ne-chee-yoh-be	Sunday	*Moku-yōbi*	moh-koo-yoh-be	Thursday
Getsu-yōbi	get-soo-yoh-be	Monday	*Kin-yōbi*	keen-yoh-be	Friday
Ka-yōbi	kah-yoh-be	Tuesday	*Do-yōbi*	doh-yoh-be	Saturday

I'm quick and I'm spry
Like a brave *samurai*.
Bamboo swings high and low
As I practice *kendo*.

Japanese word:	Sounds like. . .	And it means. . .
samurai	sam-ur-i	warrior
kendo	ken-doh	traditional sword play

I take off my shoes
When I enter the house.
On the floor as you'll see
Are straw mats – *tatami*.

Japanese word:	Sounds like. . .	And it means. . .
tatami	tah-tah-me	rice straw mat

I study hard after school
To get homework done.
Only then am I free
To watch *terebi*.

Japanese word:	Sounds like. . .	And it means. . .
terebi	teh-leh-be	television

I like to buy jeans.
To get my new clothes,
My *okāsan* and I go
To our town's *depāto*.

Japanese word:	Sounds like. . .	And it means. . .
okāsan	okah-sahn	mother
otosan	oh-to-sahn	father
depāto	day-pah-toh	department store

My goodness, the cost
Is a thousand and ten!
But that's less than it sounds
'Cause my *okane* is *yen*.

Japanese word:	Sounds like. . .	And it means. . .
okane	oh kah-neh	money
yen	yen	Japanese currency

Since we live by the sea,
Meals of *sushi* are nice.
I like *sukiyaki*,
Served with heaps of white rice.

Japanese word:	Sounds like. . .	And it means. . .
sushi	su-she	raw fish and rice
sukiyaki	su-kee-ah-kee	sliced beef with vegetables

I pick up a shrimp
Cooked with onions and peas.
I dip this meal in a sauce
Using sticks called *hashi*.

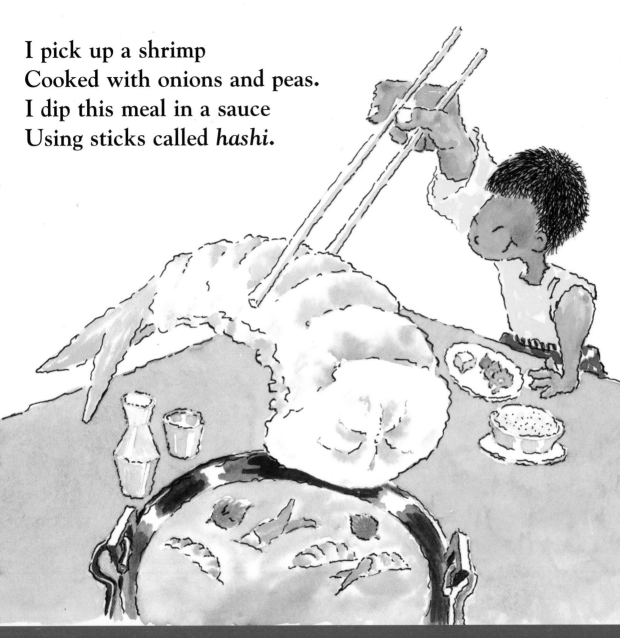

Japanese word:	Sounds like. . .	And it means. . .
hashi	hah-she	chopsticks

For fast food that I buy,
I say, *"Hanbāgā kudasai."*
Then I add to my order
A soft drink, a cold *kōra.*

Japanese word:	Sounds like. . .	And it means. . .
Hanbāgā kudasai.	hahn-bah-gah koo-dah-si	I'd like a hamburger.
kōra	kol -ah	cola

Hai, I like candy.
It's sweet, rich and *choko*.
Should I have more?
Iie, my stomach is sore!

Japanese word:	Sounds like. . .	And it means. . .
Hai	hi	yes
Iie	ee-eh	no
choko	cho-ko	chocolate

My friends and I play
With *batto* and *bōru*.
Do you like it too?
This sport's called *yakyū*.

Japanese word:	Sounds like. . .	And it means. . .
batto	bah-toh	bat
bōru	bo-lu	ball
yakyū	yahk-yoo	baseball

Who'll be first on the team?
There's no worry or fuss.
We don't fight or groan —
We simply play *jan-ken-pon*.

JAN-KEN-PON

Japanese word:	Sounds like. . .	And it means. . .
jan-ken-pon	jahn-ken-pohn	scissors-paper-rock game

I turn paper just so,
To make a white crane.
It's good fortune for me
To fold *origami*.

Japanese word:	Sounds like. . .	And it means. . .
origami	olee-gah-me	paper folding

In *haru* trees bloom.
The weather is warm.
We walk especially to see
These bright cherry *ki*.

Japanese word:	Sounds like. . .	And it means. . .
haru	hah-lu	spring
ki	kee	trees

I like Children's Day.
It's the fifth day of May.
For every small boy
Families fly a bright *koi*.

Japanese word:	Sounds like. . .	And it means. . .
koi	koy	carp fish

When I'm given a gift,
I'm polite and bow low.
I say the right words:
"*Dōmo arigatō.*"

DŌMO ARIGATŌ

Japanese word:	Sounds like. . .	And it means. . .
Dōmo arigatō	doh-moh al-e-gah-toh	Thank you

Families find time to play
On Japan's festive day.
When the year starts anew,
We enjoy *oshōgatsu*.

Japanese word:	Sounds like. . .	And it means. . .
oshōgatsu	oh-shoh-gaht-soo	New Year

I love the bright glow
Of a wrapped *kimono*.
At the waist you will see
A band — an *obi*.

Japanese word:	Sounds like. . .	And it means. . .
kimono	kee-moh-no	traditional dress
obi	oh-be	sash

We visit a temple.
What a sight to behold!
This bronze *Daibutsu*
Is five centuries old.

Japanese word:	Sounds like. . .	And it means. . .
Daibutsu	di-boots-u	Buddha

Our most famous sight
Is our high *Fuji-san*.
All year long it wears snow—
What color's the top? *Shiro*!

Japanese word:	Sounds like. . .	And it means. . .
Fuji-san	Foo-jee sahn	Mt. Fuji
shiro	sheer-oh	white

At night I unfold
A fat mat on the floor.
This bed's all my own,
And it's called a *futon*.

Japanese word:	Sounds like. . .	And it means. . .
futon	foo-tohn	mattress

Our most famous sight
Is our high *Fuji-san*.
All year long it wears snow—
What color's the top? *Shiro*!

Japanese word:	Sounds like. . .	And it means. . .
Fuji-san	Foo-jee sahn	Mt. Fuji
shiro	sheer-oh	white

At night I unfold
A fat mat on the floor.
This bed's all my own,
And it's called a *futon*.

Japanese word:	Sounds like. . .	And it means. . .
futon	foo-tohn	mattress

OYASUMI NASAI

As I drift off to sleep,
I dream of my home.
I'm so glad to have shown
You my country, *Nippon*.

Japanese word:	Sounds like...	And it means...
Nippon	neep-pohn	Japan
Oyasumi nasai	oy-ah-soo-me nah-si	Good night